RULERS, SCHOLARS, AND ARTISTS OF THE RENAISSANCE™

NICCOLÒ MACHIAVELLI

Florentine Statesman, Playwright, and Poet

RULERS, SCHOLARS, AND ARTISTS OF THE RENAISSANCE™

NICCOLÒ MACHIAVELLI

Florentine Statesman, Playwright, and Poet

Nick Ford

The Rosen Publishing Group, Inc., New York

Published in 2005 by The Rosen Publishing Group, Inc.
29 East 21st Street, New York, NY 10010

Library of Congress Cataloging-in-Publication Data

Ford, Nick.
Niccolò Machiavelli: Florentine Statesman, playwright, and poet/Nick Ford.—1st ed.
    p. cm.—(Rulers, scholars, and artists of the Renaissance)
Includes bibliographical references and index.
ISBN 1-4042-0316-8 (library binding)
1. Machiavelli, Niccolò, 1469–1527—Juvenile literature.
2. Statesmen—Italy—Florence—Biography—Juvenile literature. 3. Intellectuals—Italy—Florence—Biography—Juvenile literature. 4. Florence (Italy)—Politics and government—1421–1737—Juvenile literature.
I. Title. II. Series.
DG738.14.M2F67 2005
320.1'092—dc22

                                                    2004010570

Manufactured in the United States of America

On the cover: Background: A panorama of Florence, Italy, 1490. Inset: *Portrait of Niccolò Machiavelli* by Sandi Tito.

CONTENTS

ITALY AT THE TIME OF NICCOLÒ MACHIAVELLI

- Milan
- Pavia
- Cremona
- River Po
- Venice
- Modena
- Bologna

ROMAGNA

- Prato
- Pisa
- Florence
- Urbino
- Ragusa
- River Arno
- Perugia
- Piombino

PAPAL STATES

- Rome
- River Tiber

KINGDOM

OF

NAPLES

- Naples

Sicily

Introduction: The Mirror of the World

The aim of a comedy is to hold up a mirror.

—*A Dialogue on Language*, 1515

Niccolò Machiavelli (1469–1527) is regarded as one of the most outstanding thinkers of his age. Many people consider him a career politician whose cynical views on human nature led him to invent a theory of government in which craftiness, treachery, and ruthlessness outweigh high ideals or even the desire to do good. He is often thought of as an immoral hypocrite who sold out his youthful ideals of democracy to become a supporter and adviser of tyrants and dictators. Even his name

Niccolò Machiavelli built a political science based on humankind's unchanging nature and the cycles of history. In his lifetime, despite his reputation that followed afterward, he was a loyal patriot who loved liberty and devoted himself to his beloved Florence.

has entered the English language as a word for deviousness ("Machiavellian") and as another name for the devil ("Old Nick").

Machiavelli should not be judged so simply. In his lifetime, he made more powerful enemies than friends; however, that does not mean he was evil. In Europe, he was one of the first people we know of who studied history to learn important lessons on how people should avoid making the same mistakes as people did in the past. In his studies, he saw that nations founded on good moral principles—such as democracies—can be a cause of great evil, while governments founded on evil principles—such as dictatorships—can often do good.

Although he is best known (and often only known) for his political writings, Machiavelli was a historian, musician, and poet. He also wrote comedies that still make people laugh today. He experienced what it was like to grow up in poverty, then become famous, and then to be poor and forgotten again. He would be thrown into prison and tortured for his beliefs. Nevertheless, throughout his life, it seems Machiavelli kept a sense of humor. Although his songs and poetry are often angry or sorrowful, his comedies (or plays) reveal his preference to find things to laugh about. To him, it was always better to see the funny side of life than to weep. From his own experience of the world, it seemed to him that people who took life—and themselves—too seriously did not generally survive for long. And when Machiavelli looked for something to laugh about, no one escaped his wicked wit—he did not even spare himself.

In his histories, political works, and comedies, Machiavelli held up a mirror to the world, in which everyone—both princes and peasants—could see themselves, past and present. If people do not like what they see, and thus call it evil, is it fair to blame the man who is holding the mirror?

THE WORLD OF MACHIAVELLI

A man who wants to act virtuously in every way must come to grief among so many who are not virtuous.

—*The Prince*, 1513

Niccolò di Bernardo Machiavelli was born on May 3, 1469. He was the third child of a Florentine lawyer, Bernardo, and his wife, Bartolomea. Niccolò had two elder sisters, Primavera and Margherita. His younger brother, Totto, would follow six years later.

Although the family had many distinguished ancestors and were fairly well-off landowners in Tuscany, the branch of the family to which Bernardo belonged was poor. Bernardo's legal practice did not bring in enough

money, so he made an extra income as an editor for a firm of Florentine printers (the new technology of printing had just arrived in Florence). Bernardo would often bring pages home from the printers for correction, so young Niccolò grew up among books of all kinds, including the classics of ancient Greece and Rome, written by poets such as Homer and Virgil and historians such as Thucydides and Livy. Buying books written in Latin and Greek was his father's only extravagance. Although most professional people could read Latin and Greek, it was unusual in Renaissance Italy, despite the revival of interest in ancient Greece and Rome. These books, when they were

Florence is depicted here in 1490, during the end of Lorenzo the Magnificent's rule. Much of Florence's Renaissance architecture is due to the innovative designs of Filippo Brunelleschi. His most outstanding achievement was the dome *(center)* that tops the Cathedral of Florence, which was designed and completed between 1420 and 1446.

republished, whether hand-copied or printed, were very expensive. All these histories were the most important influence on young Niccolò in the years to come.

FLORENCE'S POLITICAL LANDSCAPE

Florence in the fifteenth century was the most prosperous and cultured city in Italy. The Italy of the fifteenth century was very different from the Italy of today. It was not one single country, but many. In the north, several city-states, such as Florence, ruled small areas. Some were republics, such as Venice, others were duchies, such as Milan, which were run by dukes. In the center of Italy, clustered around Rome, was a federation of states governed by the pope. These states were called the Papal States. To the south and including the island of Sicily, there was the kingdom of Naples, which was under French rule from 1495 until 1504, when it was taken over by the king of Spain. Gradually, Italy had become fragmented into such states since the collapse of the Roman Empire 1,000 years before.

At the time Niccolò Machiavelli was born, Italy resembled a huge battlefield. Not only were the different states frequently at war with each

This is a view of the Ponte Vecchio on the River Arno in Florence. This landmark bridge was built in the middle of the fourteenth century and at first included wool merchants' shops and grocers. However, these shops were soon considered too unsophisticated for the bridge's image and were replaced by goldsmiths and silversmiths. Today, jewelry shops are still a major feature of the bridge.

other, but, to the west, the kings of France sought to bring the smaller states, such as Florence, under French control. To the north, an empire of German and Austrian states calling itself the Holy Roman Empire also vied with France to control these little Italian states, while in the south, the king of Spain wanted to enlarge his dominions. East of Venice lay the vast empire of the Ottoman Turks, who had not yet given up on the idea of conquering all of Europe.

The republic of Florence dominated the area of northwest Italy called Tuscany, including neighboring

This is a map of sixteenth-century Europe by Italian painter Giovanni de' Vecchi (1536–1615). This fresco can be found in the Sala del Mappamondo, in the Farnese Palace in Caprarola, located in central Italy. Fresco is an ancient Roman style of painting in which pigments are applied to wet plaster directly on the wall. It was also a popular style of art during the Renaissance.

cities such as Pisa. Florence was a democracy in theory, but in practice, it was run by the Medicis, a rich and powerful aristocratic family. Positions in the government were decided by lottery—drawing the names of citizens seeking posts written on tokens from a bag—but the Medicis made sure that only their own names, and those of their supporters, went into the bag in the first place.

In 1478, when Niccolò was nine, a group of citizens, aided by Pope Sixtus IV, tried to overthrow the Medici rule. The two Medici brothers, Giuliano and Lorenzo, were attacked one morning while attending mass in the cathedral. Giuliano was killed, but Lorenzo—later known as Lorenzo the Magnificent—escaped. A subsequent attempt to topple the government of Medici supporters failed, but the pope sent an army to attack the city with the help of the king of Naples.

The Florentine army, composed mainly of mercenaries, was defeated outside the city walls, and the city was besieged. One of the chief conspirators, the pope's nephew Cardinal Riario, was taken hostage by the Florentine citizens and used as a bargaining point in the negotiations. When the Florentines released Riario, the pope broke his promise and ordered his soldiers to storm the city. Lorenzo—later to become Florence's most famous leader—saved the city and his own life by giving himself up to the king of Naples and making a separate peace with him. Without the help of his ally the king, the pope was not strong enough to continue the war against Florence. All this treachery and double-dealing probably made a strong impression on young Niccolò. For him, it was to be the first of many lessons in the deadly game of Italian politics.

Lorenzo, now leader of the city, made new laws weakening the old powers of the republic, so by 1490, he was a king in all but name. Lorenzo was an able ruler. However, the government—filled with his friends, supporters, and members of his own family—became decadent and corrupt as these people sought to benefit themselves rather than look after the well-being of the people. Only those citizens who could afford to bribe the judges had any hope of justice. The Catholic Church was corrupt in the same way as the government. Influential families simply purchased important positions for their relatives. A career in the church was seen as just another way of making money and getting more power. Without the church to give a moral lead, the city of Florence became a lawless and dangerous place. In politics and business, people simply had their rivals murdered. Young Niccolò witnessed firsthand what happened in a society without law and order, without morals or respect for authority.

THE RISE AND FALL OF THE PREACHING FRIAR

Then, when Niccolò was in his late teens, a preaching friar arrived in the city who would shake the republic from top to bottom. His name was Girolamo Savonarola. Shocked by the violence and corruption in Florence and determined to end it, he soon attracted large crowds with his eloquent preaching. He seemed to be afraid of nobody. His harshest public criticism was reserved for President Lorenzo de' Medici and for the new pope, Alexander VI, who supported him. Savonarola roused the common people to demand that their politicians and religious leaders behave like Christians. He urged everyone to shame Lorenzo and Pope Alexander VI by setting an example of decency from the bottom up. Then, he threatened, if the pope and the president still refused to lead better lives and govern justly and responsibly, God would unleash terrible punishments on the city, especially on those most responsible for its evils.

In 1492, the friar's prophecy seemed to have come true, for in a war with the Holy Roman Emperor, Lorenzo and his Florentine army were defeated and the citizens chased Lorenzo out of the city. On the advice of Savonarola, a new democratic government was created, and political and moral reforms began. This was not enough for Savonarola, who continued to denounce the pope as an evil man responsible for everything that was wrong in Christendom. In 1496, Pope Alexander VI responded by excommunicating Savonarola and ordering him to appear in Rome to answer to the Inquisition.

By this time, the people of Florence were beginning to tire of the friar's reforming zeal. They had been grateful to him for fearlessly opposing the

Girolamo Savonarola carried out the famous Bonfire of the Vanities in Florence, sending young boys door to door to collect paintings, mirrors, cosmetics, and other objects deemed sinful. The items were then burned in a large heap at the Piazza della Signoria.

tyranny and corruption in their government, but he also deemed as sinful things that many of them regarded as harmless pleasures— gambling, fine clothes, drinking, and enjoying good food and wine. His followers gradually began to desert him. Machiavelli may well have been one of these. Savonarola was arrested and handed over to the Inquisition. He was found guilty of heresy. The friar was sentenced to be hanged and then burned, probably while still alive. The execution took place in the main square of Florence, while thousands watched.

We do not know whether Machiavelli was in the crowd watching the execution, but it must certainly have made a great impression on him. It taught him that a good man such as Savonarola could change a government and better people's lives against the

The burning at the stake of Girolamo Savonarola in the Piazza della Signoria is depicted here by an unknown artist. Savonarola and two of his companions were condemned to death after being found guilty of heresy. Florence never quite regained the power and vitality that it had embodied at the time before Savonarola, when Lorenzo the Magnificent was in power. Machiavelli, who then came to work for Piero Soderini, had contempt for Savonarola's methods and ideas.

wishes of the rich and powerful, but only as long as he had the support of the common people behind him. Machiavelli saw, though, that most ordinary people are neither particularly good nor very bad since they do not tend to do more than live their lives quietly. Therefore, it was always necessary to appeal to their self-interest to keep their support.

Savonarola had taken a stand against the pope and the Medicis, and the citizens of Florence had protected him for four years. When he wanted to turn Florence into a city of saints, however, he found himself without friends. Perhaps to Machiavelli, studying his father's history books, the bad always seemed to triumph over the good, and God usually did very little to help—in fact, it seemed that God was often on the side of the bad. Machiavelli began to wonder whether lessons could be learned from history that could help prevent such tragedies in the future. Before the answers began to come to him, he would find himself close to the center of events that would make history. In 1498, just after his twenty-ninth birthday, Niccolò was elected to a high office in the republican government—an honor unheard of for someone so young and inexperienced.

SERVANT OF THE STATE

CHAPTER 2

Whenever I have had an opportunity of honoring my country, even if this involved me in trouble and danger, I have done it willingly, for a man is under no greater obligation than to his country.

—*A Dialogue on Language*, 1515

It is only from this time, when he became second chancellor to the council, that much information has come down to us about Machiavelli. From descriptions in letters and a portrait painted at about this time, we learn that Machiavelli was pale-skinned, of medium height, with an upright posture and an air of confidence. His hair was black and cut short, and his features were pointed.

He had a long nose, bright, dark eyes, and a large, high forehead, which people at that time believed to be a sign of great intelligence. His mouth always drooped slightly at the corners, as if he was deliberately trying not to smile at some secret thought that amused him.

The government post to which he was elected was a very senior one, usually reserved for much older men with wide experience of the world and, usually, a university degree. Machiavelli had none of these qualifications. How did he get the job? His family was not rich and influential. Perhaps it was because somebody spotted his talent.

Few clues shed light on how this happened. A letter about an important lawsuit sent the previous year, in 1497, to the cardinal of Perugia on behalf of the whole Machiavelli family was written by Niccolò—even though his father, Bernardo, was a doctor of law and Niccolò had no qualifications. What is still more surprising is that Niccolò's letter seems to have won the case for his family. Even at age twenty-nine, he was a powerful negotiator and an eloquent persuader among older, more experienced men.

We also know that when Machiavelli was at school he had been taught by a man named Marcello Adriani, who, by this time, was the first chancellor of the republic. Adriani was probably so impressed by young Niccolò's abilities that he recommended him for the job.

All the business of the government of the republic of Florence was handled by two chancelleries, or departments. The First Chancellery dealt with internal affairs, and the Second Chancellery, which Machiavelli had been chosen to run, dealt with foreign affairs.

At first, Machiavelli's main tasks were to write reports for briefing the council on the war with the city of Pisa, which had broken away from Florentine control. His earliest known work, *The Discourse on the Pisan War* (1498), shows that Machiavelli already had a firm grasp of political and military matters.

ENVOY TO FRANCE

All the states in northern Italy took sides in the war. One of Machiavelli's duties was to act as an envoy, a special representative of his government, to these other countries to observe and report on how their leaders reacted to the war, and either gain or improve their support through negotiation. Then in 1499, Louis XII, king of France, invaded northern Italy. One by one, the city-states fell to

King Louis XII triumphantly enters Genoa in 1499, assisted by four cardinals, after the northern Italian city-state fell to his army. Machiavelli would later use King Louis XII as an example of how not to rule in *The Prince*, pointing out various mistakes the French king made in his attempt to conquer all of Italy.

his armies, including the most powerful among them, the duchy of Milan.

On Machiavelli's advice, Florence allied itself with France, which meant the French army would help it recapture Pisa. Machiavelli was sent with the army to report to the council on the progress of the war. The war was a disaster. Machiavelli described how the badly disciplined French troops—mostly Swiss mercenaries—were more interested in attacking their allies' supply wagons than in attacking Pisa. Because they had not been paid, they then mutinied, captured a senior politician accompanying Machiavelli, and held him for ransom. Machiavelli had orders to escape back to Florence and tell the government what had happened. The council then sent him on a special mission to France to complain to King Louis XII.

It was a long and difficult journey. Before Machiavelli and his group left Italy, they had to get past a thousand of the same troops who had kidnapped Machiavelli's companion at Pisa. When they arrived in France, they found that the king and his court were always on the move to avoid an outbreak of the plague.

When at last they caught up with the French court, Machiavelli told the king that his mercenaries were roaming around in Tuscany, doing

The bubonic plague originated in the Far East and by 1350 had spread throughout Europe, mainly by merchant ships from the Mediterranean that brought the disease from the Middle East. Throughout the fifteenth and sixteenth centuries, there were periodic outbreaks in Europe. This detail from an allegorical painting depicts the devastation of the plague and war.

whatever they pleased, and that Florence, his ally in the war, would be ruined if the king did not pay the soldiers and send them home. However, King Louis XII refused to listen. Machiavelli's companions gave up and returned to Florence, but Machiavelli stayed with the French court, even though his money was running out. He was determined to do what he could for his country. He carefully observed meetings between King Louis and the envoys from the kingdom of Naples and the Papal States, which were enemies of Florence. He then smuggled his reports back to Florence.

It became clear to Machiavelli that Pope Alexander VI and his son Cesare Borgia, the Duke of Romagna, were planning with France to conquer all of Italy and divide it between them. With both France and the pope against Florence, there seemed to be little hope. Due to his tireless efforts, however, Machiavelli succeeded in persuading King Louis XII to order his armies and those of the pope not to harm the republic of Florence. The chief French negotiator, Cardinal d'Amboise, mockingly told Machiavelli: "You Italians do not understand war." Machiavelli replied, "You French don't understand politics—if you did, you would never have allowed the Church to become so powerful."

FENDING OFF CESARE BORGIA

In the spring of 1501, Machiavelli returned home. Cesare Borgia, making war against the city-state of Bologna, marched his army through Florentine territory, almost to the walls of the city itself. There he halted for a while and offered an alliance with Florence in return for a huge sum of money and a return to Medici rule. It was a thinly veiled threat. Florence had no army at the time and could not resist; however, an order from the king of France warned the duke off just in time. Machiavelli had saved his republic.

That summer, Machiavelli was busy making alliances with neighboring states that had not sided with the Borgias. He somehow found time to court and marry Marietta Corsini, but he had little time to settle into family life because war always seemed imminent. Cesare captured nearby

Piombino, a little state under Florence's protection, to enlarge his dukedom, while Piero de' Medici, his ally, led some of the duke's troops into Pisa. Then, to the east, the state of Urbino fell to the duke's soldiers, and Florence was completely surrounded by enemies. Duke Cesare ordered Florence to send him a citizen with whom he could discuss matters of great importance—he would not elaborate, but it

Cesare Borgia was exiled to Spain in 1504, where he became a soldier under the reign of his brother-in-law, King Jean d'Albret of Navarre. He died during a battle at the age of thirty-one. Today, many historians believe he was the subject of *The Prince.*

was not hard to guess that he wanted to discuss Florence's surrender. While messages were sent to King Louis XII for help, Machiavelli was ordered to the court of Duke Cesare Borgia.

The duke arrogantly told Machiavelli: "This government of yours does not please me . . . you must change it. And if you do not wish to have me as a friend, you will find me your enemy." He gave them only four days to make up their minds. Fortunately, before their time was up, a French army arrived in Florence. Under this threat, Cesare ordered his forces out of Florentine territory. King Louis XII had finally realized the truth of what Machiavelli had said at the court—that the church, under the Borgias, had become too powerful. The pope, with his own army, could do as he wished, like any other head of state. The same was true for Duke Cesare—and it seemed no other government in Europe had the political will to stop the Borgias from bringing all the states of Italy under papal rule.

Machiavelli was both repelled and impressed by Cesare Borgia as a leader: he admired Cesare's energy and intelligence but hated his ruthless ambition and cruelty. The duke was known to make public examples of all who opposed him with shocking executions. Even though they were very different, the duke found Machiavelli interesting company and spent a lot of time in conversation with him. Machiavelli took advantage of this to try and get inside the mind of Florence's most feared enemy.

Cesare Borgia wanted Florence to make him its military leader. Machiavelli was under instructions from his government to delay an official reply as long as possible, but after several months, he had to refuse. He cunningly said that Florence could not afford to give Borgia such a large commission but that it did not want to offend him by offering a small one.

Machiavelli's reports back to Florence had to be written in code to fool Borgia's spies. It was not an obvious code of mixed numbers and letters, which would immediately arouse suspicion, but one using the names of foods or articles of clothing, which had been agreed upon in advance with the Florentine government, to stand for important places and people. Cesare Borgia, for example, was sometimes referred to as a velvet hat. That way, the letters seemed homely and unimportant to those who did not know the code.

Despite Machiavelli's many requests to be allowed to return to his wife in Florence, the republic insisted that Machiavelli stay with Borgia on his campaigns to try and second-guess what he—the most dangerous man in Italy—would do. Where would he attack next? This was very difficult, as Machiavelli wrote that the duke never took others into his confidence and always acted with unpredictable speed and determination, which won him victory after victory. Even so, Machiavelli did his best to predict the duke's actions and was nearly always proved right. Machiavelli was learning valuable lessons in the ruthlessness of politics and war, which he would later describe in his books.

MACHIAVELLI AND DA VINCI

It was not until 1502 that Machiavelli was allowed to return home, and with him came Cesare Borgia's chief military engineer—Leonardo da Vinci. Da Vinci made a plan to deepen Florence's river, the Arno, turning Florence into a seaport and irrigating the surrounding land to make it more fertile. Machiavelli persuaded the government to start the first part, which was to move the river away from the rebel city of Pisa. With no water and no ships to bring in supplies, Pisa would not be able to hold out, and the war that had lasted for ten years would be over. Da Vinci even designed a mechanical digging machine to help with the immense task of shifting the river twenty miles (thirty-two kilometers).

The goal of the project was not only to ruin Pisa, which blocked Florence's seaborne trade with the Mediterranean; Machiavelli and da Vinci also planned to make the river safer. The Arno was prone to sudden fierce floods, as it still is to this day, and they believed they could tame the power of the water by building a series of dams and weirs, and use its energy to drive watermills. Then, in 1503, the New World explorer, Amerigo Vespucci, came home to Florence. He had a brother, Antonio, who had held high office in the government, and his cousin Agostino was now working for Machiavelli as an assistant in the chancellery. When Amerigo talked of the wealth of the New World, they must have discussed together how rich and important Florence could become as a seaport if the city could send its own ships to the Americas.

This is a self-portrait of Leonardo da Vinci, drawn in 1513. During his investigations on how to divert the River Arno, he became fascinated with the beauty of the landscape of the area. It was during this period that he painted the *Mona Lisa*.

Unfortunately, the people put in charge of the work on the dams were incompetent, and the plan failed because they did not follow da Vinci's instructions. Some think the work might have been sabotaged by Florence's enemies. Despite Machiavelli's arguments, the government refused

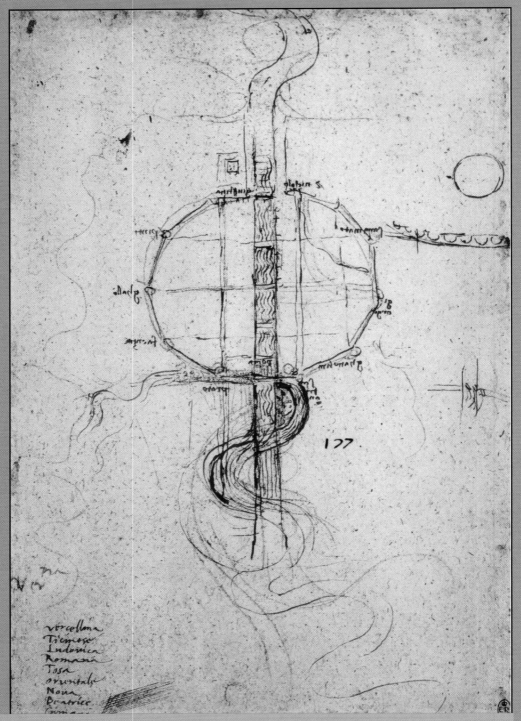

Leonardo da Vinci carefully studied the River Arno and drew up plans to divert its course. The bend in the river would be made into three channels. Although the project was abandoned at the time, a modern project closely resembles da Vinci's plans. Above is a copy of one of da Vinci's plans for the project.

to pay the money da Vinci needed to finish the job properly, and in 1506, da Vinci left the city in disgust. He and Machiavelli were never to work together again, a misfortune not only for Florence but for all of Italy.

GOOD NEWS FOR FLORENCE AND MACHIAVELLI

In the midst of this trouble, there were two consolations. The first was that in 1503, Pope Alexander VI fell suddenly ill of a fever and died. His son Cesare Borgia also became seriously ill, and although he did not die until 1507, he never recovered his powers and suffered defeat after defeat. The duke's Italian empire fell apart. Many thought that both men had been poisoned. Machiavelli was sent on a mission to Rome to report on the election of a new pope and to do his best to influence the cardinals to vote for a successor who would favor Florentine interests.

On this, his first visit to Rome, Machiavelli must have thought of the ancient city described by the Roman historians long ago—how its people had once ruled all Europe. Now most of its once magnificent buildings lay in ruins, and the city was little more than a center for the political intrigues and squabbles of cardinals and the different states and aristocratic families that backed them. On a later visit, when he would see the emperor's foreign soldiers swaggering arrogantly in the streets, he began to write down his thoughts about how history repeats itself and how mistakes made in the past can be avoided in the future.

The other good news came on Christmas Eve, 1503, when Machiavelli's wife, Marietta, wrote him that they had a son:

> My dearest Niccolò . . . the baby is doing nicely. He looks like you: skin white as snow and a head like black velvet, and hairy all over, the way you are! Since he is so like you, I suppose I must call him handsome.

Machiavelli was home in a few days. He and Marietta christened the baby Bernardino, after his grandfather.

In 1504, a rare period of peace began for all of Italy. Machiavelli was able to spend time with his family and think about what he had learned on his travels and how it could be put to good use. Having followed the mercenary armies of the king of France and Cesare Borgia, and of his own country, he saw how unreliable and untrustworthy mercenaries were. They fought for whomever would pay the highest price and were reluctant to risk their lives for anybody. By contrast, at the siege of Pisa, he had seen how bravely mere citizens could fight. Even when the work was under way to change the course of the River Arno, Florence had to pay a thousand soldiers to guard the workforce against attacks by the Pisans.

Machiavelli drew up plans for something unheard of at that time. Florence was to have its own citizen army—the militia.

MACHIAVELLI AT WAR

1
2

4
5
6
7

CHAPTER 3

The first way to lose your nation is to neglect the art of war; the first way to win a nation is to be skilled in the art of war.

—*The Prince*, 1513

Florence was to make its own citizens into soldiers instead of needing to rely on expensive hired killers from foreign countries. Government officials were opposed to the idea at first—they were not sure that they could trust the common people to bear arms—but Machiavelli convinced them with his arguments. He said that by giving citizens military training, ancient Rome had not only protected itself but had also conquered the world. During their own time, he said,

By hiring Swiss mercenaries to conduct military operations against their rivals, Italian city-states did not risk the lives of their own people. However, the use of mercenaries often prolonged wars, and mercenaries could not be relied upon for their loyalty, nor would they risk their own lives for their employer's cause.

the Swiss—a people who were free to bear arms—were among the best soldiers in Europe. An armed population was a safeguard of freedom against an unpopular government that disregarded the will of the people because no dictator would be able to rule them by force. A people used to military discipline would also have a good sense of law and order, and would be easier to govern. A well-trained and well-led army of citizens, he argued, would fight better than mercenaries because they would risk their lives to protect their homes and families. However, mercenaries cannot be relied upon to face death for just a wage. Moreover, contrary to mercenaries, an army of citizens would always be ready when needed and cheaper to maintain.

The government agreed, but who was to train and lead the militia? Machiavelli's proposal horrified them. He suggested Don Michele, former general of the despised Cesare Borgia. Machiavelli had seen him achieve great military successes with the conscripted peasants of Romagna, turning them into disciplined, reliable soldiers. Again, he persuaded the government officials to his way of thinking.

In February 1506, the new citizen army paraded in the main square, uniformed in white jackets, pants that were half red and half white, steel breastplates, and white caps. Most were armed with pikes, but some were equipped with newly invented handguns. They drilled and exercised in the Swiss fashion. Fellow citizen Luca Landucci later wrote: "It was the finest spectacle that has ever been organized in the city of Florence." A permanent board of officials was set up to administer the militia and Machiavelli ran this organization, too, for no extra pay.

In 1509, Machiavelli's militia besieged Pisa, closing all supply routes to the city. The militia had its own commanders, but the soldiers saw Machiavelli as their real general. The discipline of the army and Machiavelli's organization were so effective that after fifteen years of war, the city surrendered after only four months' siege by his new army.

Machiavelli knew that most battles cannot be won by infantry alone. In 1510, he asked the government to raise a regiment of cavalry as well. These were not to be heavily armored knights on huge horses, which were impressive but slow-moving and expensive, but mobile, lightly armed riders with guns and crossbows, ideal for scouting and for damaging the enemy at a distance before it could come up against the infantry.

THE SURGE TO WAR

In 1511, Machiavelli was busy inspecting all the fortresses in Florentine territory. It was only a matter of time before war came again. The new pope, Julius II, had been fighting to regain the Papal States, which had broken away on the death of Pope Alexander VI, and to unite all the other states of Italy. Only Florence stood against him. The cardinals who were opposed to Julius II summoned him to appear at a council in Pisa. Pope Julius II responded by placing the Florentine republic under an interdict. He had made alliances with the kings of Spain and Naples. Florence, traditionally allied with France, sent Machiavelli to the court of the Holy Roman Emperor to ask for his help.

Florence also had enemies within its borders. Aristocratic families who did not like the republic plotted with the support of Cardinal Giovanni de' Medici and Pope Julius II to assassinate the president and invite the Medicis back to rule. The government itself was divided, for many in Florence feared another war and wanted to remain neutral. Machiavelli warned that this was impossible, for then either side could attack Florence and there would be no one to help.

The rebel cardinals met in Pisa, intending to depose the pope and elect a new pope from among themselves. French troops were marching into Florence to protect it, while armies from

Pope Julius II increased the church's power through military conquests and political strategy. Machiavelli would commend him in *The Prince* for his successes, which he felt were due to his passion for his causes. Julius II was also a patron of the arts. The portrait above was painted by Raphael.

Naples, Spain, and the Papal States moved north to attack.

One stormy night, in the middle of all this uncertainty and fear, a bolt of lightning struck the palace of the government in Florence and destroyed a shield over the door bearing the design of a lily. This was seen as a terrible omen, for the lily was the emblem both of France and of Florence. Machiavelli, fearing the worst, wrote up his will and then hastily set about raising more troops for the militia, especially cavalry.

News arrived that the French general had been killed in a battle with papal forces at Ravenna, a frontier city in Romagna. Spanish troops were entering Tuscany. Machiavelli was sent with his new troops to meet the enemy but was recalled at the last minute since the government could not agree on what to do.

Machiavelli would later write that a democracy that works well in peacetime cannot fight a war efficiently unless a single leader is chosen to act as commander in chief.

The pope demanded the resignation of Florence's president, Piero Soderini. He refused, saying that the people had voted him to office, so he would resign only if they wished it. Then disaster struck. The Florentine militia met the Spanish army at Prato and was defeated. The militia fought

The lily was a flower that naturally grew along the city walls of Florence and in the nearby fields. It made its way onto the Medici family's coat of arms, a privilege the family gained from Louis XI because of diplomatic services. The lily then became the symbol of Florence and Tuscany.

well, but the new Spanish troops were the best soldiers Italy had ever seen. The cause of the republic was lost. President Soderini fled. The Medicis returned to Florence as private citizens, and the head of the opposition party, Giovanbattista

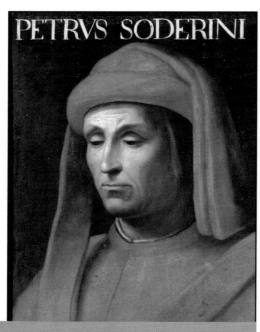

PETRVS SODERINI

When he was exiled from Florence, Piero Soderini took refuge in Ragusa until Pope Leo X was elected. From Rome, he did work to help Florence, yet he was never allowed to return to the city he once led.

Ridolfi, a relative of the Medicis', was made the new president. Shortly thereafter, rigged elections put the Medicis and their supporters into all the government offices, and piece by piece, they began to dismantle the democratic constitution of the republic. The first two actions they took were to disband the militia and fire Machiavelli, who had served the republic so well. After fourteen years, his career was in ruins and it seemed that all his work had come to nothing.

Writer in Exile

Which is the more ungrateful,
a people, or a prince?

—*The Discourses*, 1517

The Medici faction wanted not only power but revenge on those who had kept them out of the republic for so long. Machiavelli was arrested on a false charge of embezzling public money to pay for the militia and fined 1,000 gold florins. This was a huge sum that he could never have been able to pay himself, but his friends paid it for him. He was not only forbidden to leave Florentine territory but also banned from entering the palace, the center of government where he had worked so hard.

Not long afterward, Machiavelli was arrested and thrown into jail again because he was suspected of being part of a conspiracy to murder Cardinal Giovanni de' Medici. In those times, it was common for people accused of serious crimes against the state to be tortured. In theory, this was meant to prove whether they were telling the truth. In practice, though, it often meant that a prisoner would tell his torturers anything they wanted to hear, just so the torture would stop.

The chief method of torture used by the Florentine government was the strappado, for which the victim's wrists were tied behind his back, then pulled upward until his whole body was lifted off the ground, only to drop him with a sudden jerk that could dislocate the arms. Four drops of the strappado was usually more than enough for even the toughest of prisoners. Machiavelli, however, was given six—but he never told his questioners anything except that he was innocent and did not even know most of the conspirators. In February 1513, Pope Julius II died and the new pope—Cardinal Giovanni de' Medici, now Pope Leo X—celebrated his election by giving a general amnesty to all the conspirators who had not already been executed. Machiavelli, freed from prison, quietly left the city amid the fireworks and

A pen and ink depiction of the use of the strappado as torture by the Inquisition by Italian Renaissance artist Domenico Beccafumi (1486–1551). His style, with his use of emotional tension, is closely associated with the Mannerism style of art. Mannerist art took an emotional attitude toward the subject matter, unlike the Renaissance style, which emphasized balance and harmony.

celebrations. He joined his family on a little farm in the country to recover and think about what to do next. He was out of work, heavily in debt, and by now he and Marietta had more children, which meant a larger family to feed.

RETREATING TO THE COUNTRY

After so long in the city, at the center of events, life in the country seemed slow and uneventful. In the daytime, Machiavelli worked on the farm supervising the workers. Every evening, he sat down to write letters to important people—especially his friends—asking them to help him find employment at the kind of work he did so well. He refused to believe that even his enemies, the Medicis, could hate him so much that they would not want to make some use of his talents. He was to be sorely disappointed. For all the letters he wrote, no offers of work came.

Machiavelli still managed to turn even this difficult situation to his advantage. He had plenty of spare time, so he began to set in order all the notes he had made from his historical studies and his experiences of war and at the courts of Europe where he had been an emissary. In December 1513,

Castello di Bibbione, located near Florence, was begun in the year 1000. Machiavelli bought the castle in 1511 and used it as a hunting lodge. His family home was in San Andrea, about 4 miles (6 km) away. His descendants remained in possession of the ancient castle until 1727.

he wrote his friend Francesco Vettori, the Florentine ambassador to the papal court in Rome:

> When evening comes I return home and go to my study, removing at the door the dirty clothes I have worn all day, and dress in my court robes; thus properly dressed, I enter the courts of the ancients . . . I ask them the reasons for doing the things they did; and they kindly answer me . . . I forget all my troubles . . . I have written down what I have learned from their conversation and composed a short work, "The Prince."

THE PRINCE AND THE DISCOURSES

The Prince is Machiavelli's best-known and most misunderstood work. Around sixty pages long, it is in many ways a summary of his longest book, The Discourses, which he had already begun and was to spend many years finishing. While The Discourses compares the politics of his own time with the republican Rome described by the historian Livy (59 BC–17 AD), The Prince is a guidebook on governing by monarchy or dictatorship.

Although he was a republican and had suffered for his political beliefs, Machiavelli saw that Italy would always suffer from being made up of disunited states. These states would always be at the mercy of large and powerful neighboring countries until one strong leader could pull them all together. Until then, there would never be peace in Italy. The idea of a dictator disgusted him, but he hoped that one day a leader would emerge who would have the strength to unite all the people under his personal rule and also have the wisdom to turn the power over to the people, having made laws that would guarantee their security and freedom. This had happened in ancient times, he wrote, with Romulus, the founder of the republic of Rome, and with Moses, the founder of the

EXAMEN DU PRINCE

MACHIAVEL,
AVEC DES NOTES
Historiques & Politiques:

A LONDRES,
Chez GUILLAÜME MEYER,
Libraire dans le Strand,
M. D. CC. XLI.

Titelblatt zu Friedrichs des Großen berühmten Fürstenbuche „Antimachiavel".

This is an edition in French of Machiavelli's *The Prince*, printed in London in 1741. This master plan, first a gift to Lorenzo de' Medici (the grandson of Lorenzo the Magnificent) as a guide for how to gain and hold on to power, was not published until five years after Machiavelli's death. It had become more widely known by the latter part of the sixteenth century and was officially banned as a dangerous book by the Catholic Church in 1559.

A nineteenth-century artist's depiction of Machiavelli, most likely portraying him during his time of exile in San Casciano. It is said he dressed in his old robes of his days in office and spent four hours an evening writing.

nation of Israel, as well as with many others. Why should it not happen again?

Machiavelli believed that this ideal was so desirable, it would be worth doing almost anything to achieve it. He had no use for morality, because he thought that most people were weak and foolish enough to do more evil than good, no matter what their moral beliefs were. To him, the end results alone were what defined an action as good or bad. This was to become Machiavelli's revolutionary new political philosophy, expressed in *The Prince*.

His friend Vettori suggested that Machiavelli should present his new work to Pope Leo X, but Machiavelli was doubtful. This new pope was a Medici and the head of a family who seemed to hate Machiavelli personally. In addition, throughout his political career, Machiavelli had counseled the Florentine republic to stay allied to France, the traditional enemy of the papacy. Machiavelli also hated the idea of the church as a political power. In his *Discourses*, he blamed the political ambition of the popes for many of Italy's misfortunes. He did not want to risk his life by going to Rome to present *The Prince* in person.

Eventually, Vettori persuaded Machiavelli to send him the manu-

Pope Leo X was the second son of Lorenzo the Magnificent, who was the most famous member of the Medici family. Although Leo X was pious, he is remembered for his extravagance, which sometimes included banquets of sixty-five-course meals. The outrage of Martin Luther, an Augustinian friar, at Pope Leo's sale of indulgences (certificates of forgiveness), sparked the Protestant Reformation.

script of *The Prince* in Rome, and he would show it to the pope instead. Machiavelli did so, but after Vettori had read the book himself, he sent it back, saying he dared not even show such a book to the pope. Machiavelli must have been bitterly disappointed. For a long time, he stopped writing letters to his friend.

Nonetheless, Machiavelli felt that he had to try to present the book to some powerful patron who, he hoped, would be so impressed with it he would offer Machiavelli an important position as an adviser. At the same time, Machiavelli wanted to do as much good as he could for his country, so, in about 1516, he decided to present his book to the pope's nephew, Duke Lorenzo de' Medici, the grandson of Lorenzo the Magnificent, who was now the ruler of Florence. One day when the duke was holding court and receiving presents from people who wanted favors, Machiavelli arrived with his book. Someone had just given the duke a present of a pair of hunting dogs, so when the book was presented to him, he barely glanced at it but continued to pet the dogs. Barely able to contain his anger, Machiavelli left the palace and went back to his farm and his studies.

Laughter and Tears: Playwright and Novelist

1
2
3
4
6
7

CHAPTER 5

If this seems too silly for someone who likes to be thought of as serious, forgive him: for he must try, with his imagination, to make bad times seem better. He can do nothing else, because he is not allowed to show his talents in any other way.

—Prologue to *The Mandrake Root*, 1518

Machiavelli began to despair of ever being able to resume a career in politics, but he was not a man to indulge in self-pity. Even in times of trouble, his well-developed sense of humor never deserted him—even though it has caused people to misunderstand him.

Santa Croce Church was begun in 1294 and is considered a masterpiece of Gothic architecture. This was a style characterized by pointed arches and sculptural details, and the precursor to the Renaissance style of architecture.

In 1504, Machiavelli's father died. A friar told Machiavelli that when workmen opened the family vault in the church of Santa Croce in Florence for the burial, they had found that several other families had illegally buried their relatives there, too. He suggested that Machiavelli give orders for the bodies to be removed. Machiavelli replied: "Let them be, for my father always loved conversation, and the more people there are there to keep him company, the better pleased he will be."

When in prison, facing torture and a possible sentence of death, he wrote a poem in which he joked about the size of the bugs in his cell. He told stories and jokes to his neighbors in the roadside inn near his farm. He had a talent for making people laugh and was a shrewd judge of character.

It occurred to him that if no one wanted to read his serious writings, he could at least earn some money by writing comedy.

He began to spend more time in the city of Florence, where he was invited to parties at which writers, poets, and scholars gathered to enjoy each other's work. After being so rudely received by Duke Lorenzo, Machiavelli made a present of his *Discourses*, which he finished in 1517, to two of these friends. His dedication on the first page read:

> Departing from the usual practice of authors, which has always been to dedicate their works to some prince, and, blinded by ambition and greed, praise him for all his virtuous qualities when they ought to have blamed him for all kinds of shameful deeds . . . So, to avoid this mistake, I have chosen not those who are princes but those who, on account of their innumerable good qualities, deserve to be.

It is easy to see that Machiavelli regretted the way he had tried to flatter Duke Lorenzo and was relieved that he could at least be honest with his friends.

Machiavelli's writing desk can still be seen today in San Andrea in Percussina, Italy. Machiavelli owned a small farmhouse, and during his years in exile, he tended to his vineyards, played cards with friends, and wrote his famous works.

LA MANDRAGOLA

At one of his friends' parties, he read aloud his first play, a comedy called *La Mandragola* (The Mandrake Root). The play is set in Florence, and it is likely that Machiavelli drew his characters from real people in Florence at the time—just enough so that his audience thought they recognized those people, but never so much that it could actually be proved. It may even have been Machiavelli's way of getting revenge on those who had criticized or rejected him.

The Italian Renaissance had a great impact on the world of theater. One result was Commedia del Arte, an improvisational form of acting. Troupes of Italian actors traveled throughout Europe performing improvised plays. Here, a sixteenth-century Flemish painter depicts such an Italian troupe.

In the play, a young man named Callimacho falls in love with a beautiful lady who is—unfortunately for him—married and loves her husband. Her husband desperately wants children, but she has never been able to have children. The young man disguises himself as a doctor and tells the husband (a rich, old lawyer) that he can cure his wife by giving her a secret potion to drink, made from a mandrake root, which will make her able to have children. He then proceeds to manipulate the woman until she has fallen in love with him, and soon she is pregnant. The husband, who has total faith in the young man, is happy to hear he will finally be a father, but the real father is, of course,

Callimacho. The play then ends happily for all the characters, for everyone thinks they have gotten their own way by deceiving someone else, even though they themselves have been deceived and do not realize it.

The play may have shocked some people, but it was a great success. Machiavelli tried to show that morality alone does not make people happy, but if trickery does make everyone happy and no one is hurt, then morals must be useless and trickery must be good, because it brings a good result when morality does not. Such practical, if immoral, logic is typical of Machiavelli, and in a different way, this point is also made in *The Prince* and *The Discourses*. Whether he believed it himself or not is hard to say. Ever since the times of ancient Greece, philosophers had enjoyed using logic to prove statements that everyone knew were untrue. Machiavelli may have been following this tradition, since it was another aspect of the ancient classical world that the scholars of the Renaissance were rediscovering and reintroducing into European culture.

Machiavelli was pleased to receive public recognition for his wit and humor from the people of Florence, when he could not get recognition from the aristocrats with his serious political works. Many modern critics regard *La Mandragola* as one of the best Italian plays ever written.

BELFAGOR

Encouraged by this success, Machiavelli tried his hand at writing a novel, *Belfagor*. The story begins in hell. Most people who wind up there seem to be married men who blame their fate on their wives. The rulers of hell decide to send a devil to Earth to find out if it is really true that most men in hell are there because of women. The Archdevil Belfagor is chosen to go on this mission. He is changed into human form and arrives in the guise of a handsome, rich young man in the city of Florence. His first task is to get married and see what happens. He actually falls in love with his wife, but she makes him so miserable that he runs back to hell for some peace and quiet.

People still love the tale of *Belfagor*, and it has been made into an opera and a movie. Some scholars have wondered if Machiavelli wrote it because he was beginning to hate married life himself, but nothing of Machiavelli's can be taken at face value. He and his wife, Marietta, had eight children, and many affectionate letters between them and the children survive, so it seems that he was happy with his family.

Portrait of Maddalena Doni by Raphael in 1506. Maddalena was the wife of a merchant, Agnoli Doni, who also had his portrait painted by this celebrated painter and architect of the Renaissance. Raphael studied the style of Leonardo da Vinci, as is evident here with its semblance to the *Mona Lisa*. During the Renaissance, women sought the same individuality and knowledge to better themselves as did men.

Belfagor was probably only one of many stories Machiavelli made up to amuse his friends, but sadly it is the only one he ever published.

CLIZIA

Later, in 1524, even though his fortunes were on the mend and he would once again be busily working for the Florentine government, he found time to write another play. *Clizia* was based on a comedy by the best-known ancient Roman playwright, Plautus.

It is about a son and a father who both fall in love with the same girl. In the end, the father is fooled by a young manservant dressed up like the young girl.

Clizia was first performed at a splendid banquet given by a rich citizen for the leading members of the government and other wealthy and powerful people. It was as big a hit as *La Mandragola*, and its fame spread rapidly.

This time, the play really does tell us something about Machiavelli. By then, he was fifty-five years old and had fallen in love with a pretty, young singer named Barbera, who sang the songs he composed to be performed during the interludes between the acts of his plays. She was young enough to be his daughter, and he would spend a lot of time with her when in town. In the play, the old man who makes a fool of himself by chasing a girl half his age is called Nicomaco. The name's similarity to Niccolò Machiavelli can hardly be a coincidence. He knew perfectly well that the lovely Barbera preferred men her own age, for he said so in a poem that he wrote to her:

> I can't complain of you:
> The blame is all my due;
> For I can see, it's true
> Such beauty, so sublime,
> Must love youth in its prime.

Whether he wrote about history, politics, comedies, or poems, Machiavelli wrote about people as he believed they really were, and when he criticized or made fun of their actions, he was honest enough not to overlook anyone, even if some of them were so powerful he did not dare name them. He seemed to have no illusions about the world or himself.

Historian and Papal Adviser

Time sweeps everything along and can bring good as well as evil, evil as well as good.

—*The Prince*, 1513

When Duke Lorenzo died in 1519, few people in Florence mourned. He had married a foreigner, an unpopular French princess. He had been arrogant and had ruled like a dictator, surrounded by only a few favorites, treating the republican traditions of Florence and its leading citizens with contempt. Before he was even buried, his uncle, Cardinal Giulio de' Medici, hastened from Rome to try his best to improve the reputation of the Medici family, which Lorenzo's stupidity and

Machiavelli is depicted here in middle age. He wrote the *History of Florence* between 1520 and 1527. After presenting the first eight books to Pope Clement VII, he received 120 ducats and encouragement to continue. Machiavelli approached the history as a politician seeking the truth, while at the same time avoiding offending his powerful patrons.

arrogance had lost for them. Giulio restored some of the democratic institutions and made sure that government officers were appointed on merit, not through bribery or family influence. In the spring of 1520, some of Machiavelli's friends arranged for him to meet the cardinal, who had taken an interest in his historical writings and inquired of Machiavelli's works in progress.

By then, Machiavelli was writing *The Art of War*, which like all his other political works, was based on his careful observation of recent events—including his experiences running the militia—as well as on the lessons of history. The cardinal was impressed by his work and thought he could profit by employing Machiavelli's talents.

Through the influence of his friends and the cardinal, Machiavelli was paid a salary by the government to write an official history of the republic. The wages were only about half of what he had earned as chancellor, but at last he had secure employment and recognition of his talents.

His first task as the official historian, assigned by the cardinal, was to write a discussion of Florentine politics and events from the death of Lorenzo the Magnificent to the present day. The cardinal's plan was to present the work to Pope Leo X, who needed advice on how Florence should be governed. Both the pope and the cardinal were getting old and had no sons to follow them. The Medici dynasty was coming to an end.

Typically, Machiavelli gave the advice he thought best for his country and not what he thought the pope wanted to hear. He advised that when the pope and the cardinal died, Florence should be made a free, democratic republic once more.

Machiavelli took more pride in serving his country in this way than in the offers of distinguished and well-paid employment that now began to come to him. He refused an offer from the republic of Ragusa to become its chief secretary. And when General Prospero Colonna, who had commanded the armies of the pope and the king of France, asked Machiavelli to work for him as his secretary for twice his old salary as secretary and five times more than the government was paying him as its official historian, he turned down that offer as well.

Later, the government found another small task for Machiavelli, which again he did not refuse, although they may have expected him to do so. He was sent as ambassador to the convention of the order of the Franciscan friars, which was in session at Carpi, near Modena, to ask that the branches of the order in Florence be made independent of the others in the region. He also asked that a friar be sent to preach in the cathedral. His old friend Francesco Gucciardini, a fellow Florentine and former ambassador, was now living in nearby Modena as governor of the Papal States. On his way to the friars, Machiavelli visited his friend and arranged to play a joke on them. Every day, the governor sent soldiers on horseback with urgent letters for Machiavelli, who pretended they were important diplomatic dispatches. The friars would stop whatever they were doing and crowd around Machiavelli, anxious to hear the news. Machiavelli would pretend to read from the letters, talking about secret international treaties and invasions, when in fact all the letters contained was trivial chat from Gucciardini.

Machiavelli would sit down, looking as serious as he could manage, and write a chatty reply telling his friend how impressed the friars were and how they could not do enough for him to make him comfortable. He would then solemnly seal his letter and hand it to the soldiers, who would salute and gallop back to the governor as if it were a national emergency. On one day, Gucciardini even sent his dispatch riders twice, and Machiavelli begged him to stop before the friars became suspicious and saw through the joke.

On his return to Florence, he made his report to the council, then withdrew from the city once more with his small library of books and papers to his little farm in the country to continue writing *The History of Florence.* It was to keep him occupied for the next seven years, almost to the time of his death.

NEW LEADERS, NEW TURMOIL

Machiavelli did not get a great deal of peace for study and writing. Late in 1521, Pope Leo X died, and in June 1522, Cardinal Giuliano de' Medici was assassinated by people known to be influential friends of Machiavelli's. The new pope, Adrian VI, had them arrested and imprisoned. Suspicion pointed at Machiavelli, but he was cleared after an investigation, though it could not have been an easy time for him. His friends were in jail, he was under suspicion of being what today we would call a terrorist, and the new pope did not think well of him. The same year, the plague ravaged the city of Florence. Among the victims was his brother, Totto, who had become a priest. His old patron and friend Piero Soderini, the former president of the republic whom he had served as secretary, also died.

In 1523, Pope Adrian VI died unexpectedly and Cardinal Giulio de' Medici of Florence was elected as the new pope, Clement VII. Machiavelli was now able to present the first eight volumes of his history to the pope after all—to the man who had commissioned Machiavelli to write it in the first place.

Machiavelli's political advice, written in his history of Florence, was now needed more than ever by the pope. Florence's traditional ally, France, had been badly defeated at the Battle of Pavia, and the

Pope Adrian VI was from the Netherlands, and during his twenty-month term as pope, he tried to restore the papacy that had been damaged by the lavishness of Pope Leo X.

French king, François I, was the prisoner of Charles V, king of Spain and the Holy Roman Emperor. The papacy had allied itself with France, too, and now Emperor Charles V, with his armies victorious in Italy and no one to stop them, regarded both the pope and Florence as his enemies. Forced to make a humiliating treaty with Charles V, Pope Clement VII ordered Cardinal Salviati as his representative to the emperor's court to negotiate its terms. The cardinal

This is a papal ducat of Pope Clement VII. Minting coins was the sovereign right of the papacy. The ducat was originally the currency of the Venetian republic, as the florin was the official currency of Florence.

asked the pope if Machiavelli could go with him and advise him, but for some reason, the pope refused. It was unlikely that he was angry with Machiavelli, for when the first volumes of the history of Florence were presented to him, he gave Machiavelli a rich bonus of 120 ducats from his personal treasury. It seems more probable that he either wanted Machiavelli close by to advise him or that he was afraid Machiavelli would give the emperor good advice instead.

Pope Clement VII was in a very difficult position. Charles V was threatening to conquer all of Italy, while the king of France was in prison at his mercy. The only king who could possibly send an army to help was King Henry VIII of England.

In the Battle of Pavia on February 24, 1525, the French army of 28,000 men was nearly wiped out by the Spanish counterattack. François I was taken prisoner, and in Madrid, he surrendered French claims in Italy. This battle marked the beginning of Spanish dominance in Italy, which lasted until the early eighteenth century.

Although England was now on friendly terms with France, Henry had never liked King François I. Besides, Henry's queen, Catherine of Aragon, was the emperor's aunt, and he did not want to anger her powerful family for the sake of a small state in Italy.

MACHIAVELLI'S ADVICE IGNORED

Pope Clement VII could not raise an army to fight the emperor because he had no money to pay for soldiers. He had no money because, unlike previous popes, he refused to sell important church offices

· ANNO · ETATIS ·   · SVÆ · XLIX ·

Henry VIII was the King of England from 1509 to 1547. It was his obsession with producing a male heir that would bring about the separation of the Church of England from Roman Catholicism. Pope Clement VII denied the king a divorce from Catherine of Aragon because the pope was obliged to Charles V—the Holy Roman Emperor and the nephew of Catherine.

to pay for the cost of war. Instead, he asked for Machiavelli's help.

Machiavelli suggested that the pope raise a national militia instead of having to buy mercenary soldiers, as he had previously persuaded the Florentine republic to do. However, he warned that it would take at least two years before they were properly equipped and trained.

The pope hesitated to take Machiavelli's advice because the pope's counselors said that while ordinary citizens would fight for their country, they would not risk their lives for a pope. Machiavelli, tired of the pope's indecisiveness, made excuses that he was needed at home and returned to Florence to continue his histories.

Now that the pope was openly asking for Machiavelli's advice, the government thought it safe to revoke the ten-year-old ban on Machiavelli taking part in political activities, and his salary as official historian was doubled. He was also sent on a minor diplomatic mission to Venice, investigating a fraud case in which some Florentine merchants were the victims. Although petty and unchallenging compared to the important missions he had previously carried out in the courts of Europe, it was better than nothing. At least he was being asked to do something for his fellow countrymen, and it was another chance to see a little more of the world and its people, from whom he was always able to learn. He had also been asked privately by Francesco Vettori, the Florentine ambassador in Rome, to speak with the papal ambassador in Venice, so it is possible that his trip to help the merchants was a cover for something far more important and highly secretive.

Even so, it must have been exasperating for Machiavelli to have his advice ignored by the pope—the one man who could save Italy from foreign domination—and to know that his country was in grave danger. Although he could do a great deal to help as he had done before, this was the best use his government would make of him. Soon, though, they would turn to him again for help—but by then, it would be too late.

THE FINAL YEARS

I love my country more than
my very soul. I can tell you
this, with sixty years of
experience behind me: we
have never been in a more
difficult situation than this,
where peace is needed, but
war cannot be avoided.

—Letter to Francesco
Vettori, April 16, 1527

CHAPTER 7

In 1526, King François I was
released by the emperor, after agree-
ing to surrender all his interests in
Italy and to pay the emperor a small
fortune. No one in Italy expected
the French king to keep his word to the
emperor, so once more the states of
Italy prepared for war. Machiavelli

King François is credited for bringing the Renaissance to France. Though the kings before him had fought wars with Italy, they were not as interested in bringing back the intellectual movement happening there. François convinced Leonardo da Vinci to move to France. The king was also responsible for the rebuilding of the Louvre and providing it with masterpieces from the king's private collection, as well as from those of the kings before him.

was sent to help Count Navara, a famous military engineer, oversee the defenses of Florence. He was instructed to report directly to the pope and advise him in person. Soon after, Machiavelli was chosen as secretary and quartermaster to the government's new defense department, with his eldest son, Bernardino, as his assistant.

Florence, the republic of Venice, and the pope made an agreement with the king of France to attack the imperial forces in Italy. They decided that they could not afford to wait for French soldiers to arrive. The Florentine army marched on the duchy of Milan, which was then under imperial control. With them went Machiavelli. He reorganized the militia, which had been raised once more but was in poor shape. He wrote many letters and reports home, which were eagerly read. He also went to the Venetian army, which was then besieging Cremona, to advise them on strategy.

Meanwhile, the emperor's forces in the south outmaneuvered the pope, who had to shut himself up in his fortress of Sant'Angelo in Rome, while imperial soldiers looted and burned the city. Finally, the pope had to surrender. When the news came, Machiavelli went to the commander of the papal forces in Romagna to discuss their chances of success if they continued to fight.

The Florentine, Venetian, and papal armies in the north were beaten, and their general, Giovanni de' Medici, was killed. The emperor's victorious German and Spanish troops advanced south to Florence. What was left of the Florentine army, thanks partly to Machiavelli's efforts, rallied and hurried to defend Florence from the invaders. Machiavelli, remaining with what was left of the papal army in Romagna, wrote his wife and children on the farm, warning them to leave with what food and possessions they could gather for the greater safety of Florence's city walls. He promised to join them as soon as he could.

Inside the city of Florence, the people were hostile to the Medici rulers, whom they blamed for their misfortune. They were angry, too, at being forced to pay extra taxes for the mercenary soldiers, whose behavior toward them, they said, was little better than the enemy's. The citizens refused to let these foreign hired troops inside their walls. They demanded arms so they could defend themselves. Rumors flew about that the Medicis were planning to leave the city to its fate. Angry mobs demonstrated outside the palace, then broke in and occupied it, throwing the Medici supporters out. Those inside the palace soon found themselves besieged by soldiers loyal to the Medicis. The whole city was on the brink of revolution.

Fortunately, when the imperial army came close, its general, seeing the allied army outside the city and the size and strength of the city's fortifications with armed citizens manning the battlements, decided instead to take his army to Rome, which he hoped would be an easier target. It was. The pope's soldiers were nowhere to be seen, and within two hours, the holy city was full of imperial troops—Protestant Germans and Catholic Spaniards alike—looting, killing, and raping while the pope could only watch helplessly from Castel Sant'Angelo.

When the news arrived in Florence that the Medici pope was finished as a political force, the revolution occurred. A council was formed, which restored the democratic institutions of the old republic as it had been when Machiavelli was elected to serve as its youngest chancellor. The Medicis, now reduced to the rank of ordinary citizens, chose to leave.

THE END OF A PROLIFIC POLITICAL CAREER

What happened next was a bitter blow for Machiavelli. Although he had served the old republican government so well and for so long—and suffered imprisonment, torture, and poverty because of his

This is a view of the Castel Sant'Angelo in Rome from the bridge over the River Tiber, as it appears today. Its first purpose was to be a mausoleum for the Roman emperor Hadrian (76–138 AD) and his successors, but later it became a fortress for the popes when it was attached to the Vatican with a special secret passageway.

opposition to the Medicis—the new republican government did not recall him to office. Instead, officials confirmed in his place a man who had been appointed under the Medicis. Perhaps they distrusted Machiavelli for having worked his way into the Medicis' favor and blamed him for Pope Clement VII's failures.

The citizens rejoiced in the streets at their country's newfound freedom, but not Machiavelli. Nearly sixty, he was feeling very old, tired, and disappointed. The past year of war and his constant traveling on missions and campaigns that would have exhausted a much younger man had made him very ill. He complained of terrible stomach pains. A special medicine that he recommended to his friend Gucciardini two years earlier, saying it had brought him back to life, only made him worse, no matter how much of it he took. He began to realize he was dying.

When his friends came to visit him to say goodbye, he told them a story. He said he had had a dream in which he saw all the souls who had ever lived on the earth being divided into two groups: one going up to heaven and the other going down to hell. An angel asked him which group he wanted to go with. He told the angel that, since he had seen that all the scholars and thinkers of ancient Greece and Rome were in the group going to hell, that he would prefer to go with them—without them in Heaven, he joked, he would be bored for the rest of eternity. Soon after, on June 22, 1527, his son Piero, age thirteen, wrote to his maternal uncle Francesco:

> I can only weep as I have to tell you that Niccolò, our father, died here on this 22nd of stomach pains caused by a medicine he took on the 20th. He allowed Brother Matteo, who was with him to the last, to

Here, patients are visiting a physician's office. During the time of the Renaissance, many medical diagnoses were made after examining the fluids of the body. Sickness was seen as an imbalance of these fluids, leading a doctor to bleed the patient (as seen above) or induce vomiting.

hear his confession. Our father, as you know, left us in direst poverty. When you come back this way I shall have a great deal to tell you. Just now I am in a great hurry and can say no more.

The next day, Niccolò Machiavelli, having died at age fifty-eight, was buried in the family church of Santa Croce in Florence, where his tomb can still be seen today.

A MAN AHEAD OF HIS TIME

As with so many other great men and women in history, Machiavelli and his work became much better known after his death. His most famous book, *The Prince*, by which most people unfairly judge him, did not appear in public until 1532, a year after the publication of his *Discourses.*

Both books seemed to upset nearly everyone who read them. Even though Pope Clement VII had allowed them to be printed, after he died in 1534, the new pope, Paul III, forbade anyone living in the Papal States to buy or sell them. In 1559, they were placed on the Index of Prohibited Books, a list of books no Catholic was allowed to read. True, Machiavelli had criticized the church and its leaders, blaming them for much that was wrong in society and for deviating from the teachings of Jesus in the Bible. He never criticized the Bible: he only pointed out that morality and politics had nothing to do with each other, because in politics, it is often necessary to do immoral things in order to bring about a good government that is strong enough to last. He believed that religion was good insofar as it served the state, and the state gave people peace, prosperity, and security. He was accused of being a pagan—that is, believing in the religion of the ancient Romans—because he expressed his admiration for the religious virtues of ancient Rome that led people to sacrifice their personal wishes for the well-being of their country. It was a religion that concentrated on improving this world, rather than on being happy in the next.

A handwritten page from Machiavelli's *Discourses*. This work is considered to be a broader, deeper look into Machiavelli's politics and beliefs than *The Prince*, for which he is most often judged and criticized. His passion for the form of government of ancient Rome is evident, as the heroes of this work are the ancient Roman people.

Even in Protestant countries such as Germany and England, Machiavelli's condemnation of what the Catholic Church had become did not gain him any public admirers. They did not like to think of the world as Machiavelli described it—a place where people were at least partially responsible for what happened to them. Although Catholics believed in free will, Protestants held the belief that all things that happened were the will of God. In Protestant countries Machiavelli was accused of being an atheist because he taught that humans, and not God, caused events to occur.

The way in which Machiavelli described human nature and its weaknesses—and how effective it was to exploit people's weaknesses, even for their own good in the long run—was too brutally honest for most people to handle. Far more people were ready to condemn Machiavelli than they were to read him. The word "Machiavellian," meaning "full of evil cunning," first entered the English language in 1568. In his play *Henry VI*, William Shakespeare makes the villain Richard III refer to himself as being craftier than Machiavelli. But there were always those who found that Machiavelli's ideas made good sense.

In 1538, the exiled English bishop Cardinal Pole— a relative and an enemy of Henry VIII's—claimed, in an essay he dedicated to the Emperor Charles V, that in 1529, Thomas Cromwell, one of King Henry VIII's chief advisers, had acquired a handwritten copy of Machiavelli's *The Prince* when in Italy. He had showed it to Henry VIII on his return to England, recommending it as a useful textbook for a ruler to follow.

Bishop Stephen Gardiner, another of Henry VIII's most trusted advisers and later chancellor to Henry's daughter Queen Mary, wrote a guidebook for King Philip II of Spain on how to govern England when he married Queen Mary. All the ideas in the book are Machiavelli's, and in it there are many quotations from Machiavelli's *The Prince* and *The Discourses*, although Machiavelli is not mentioned anywhere in the book. Gardiner used examples from English history to illustrate those ideas in the way Machiavelli had used recent Italian history as well as ancient Greek and Roman history. Not only does this show that Gardiner had read Machiavelli and thought his ideas were sound, but the passages in the book, which give examples of Henry VIII's cleverness as a ruler, strongly suggest that Henry had studied Machiavelli and put his ideas into practice.

Pole thought that this proved that Machiavelli and Henry were both evil men, while Gardiner thought it showed that they had learned the secrets of efficient governing. Machiavelli knew firsthand the sufferings of countries with weak governments, like the states of Italy, and could contrast them with his experience of countries with strong governments, like France. He saw that a strong government might not always be good in itself, but it was far better than a weak government, which—though it might not be evil—certainly led to many evils, such as the instability and weakness that destroyed the republics of Athens, ancient Rome, and his own Florence.

Machiavelli himself, in a letter to his friend Vettori, once described Henry VIII as "cruel and ambitious." For the most part, he did not like princes and preferred republics. Although he has been called devious and hypocritical for writing *The Prince*, which praises monarchy, for a Medici autocrat, and writing *The Discourses*, which praises republicanism, for his friends, we must remember that in both books the ideas are the same. Machiavelli was desperate to put his ideas across to anyone who would listen because he knew that without such ideas, Italy was in danger.

But it was not until a century and a half later that a widespread interest in Machiavelli began. By the second half of the eighteenth century, the development of scientific theory in Europe and America

The tomb of Niccolò Machiavelli is located in the church of Santa Croce in Florence, Italy. A few weeks before his death, he wrote to a good friend that he loved his fatherland more than his own soul. Only in recent years has this devoted statesman's reputation evolved into one of deeper respect. This is a result of his writings being better understood.

Italian nationalist Giuseppe Garibaldi succeeded in 1865 at what Machiavelli dreamed of 300 years earlier—Italian unification. Venice was added to the kingdom in 1866, followed by Rome, which became its capital in 1871.

had begun to replace religion in people's minds as the foundation of how nations should be governed. Those who took up his ideas were republicans such as Alexander Hamilton, James Madison, and John Adams. Machiavelli's description in *The Discourses* of the republic of ancient Rome, as combining the three best aspects of democracy, oligarchy, and monarchy, probably influenced the authors of the Constitution of the United States.

In the nineteenth century, the professional Italian soldier Giuseppe Garibaldi fulfilled Machiavelli's ideal of a united Italy, liberated from foreign rulers by a patriot willing to use any means to achieve it. However, not until 1946, 419 years after Machiavelli's death, did his dream of a united

Italian republic become a reality. The man who had seen the future of his country in a vision inspired by the ancient Rome of 2,000 years before was truly a man born ahead of his time.

Nowadays, Machiavelli's works are required reading in many university courses on politics and history, while his plays and his novel are read and performed by students of literature and drama of the Italian Renaissance. His works can be found in libraries and bookstores around the world, and there are appreciation societies, Web sites, and even chat rooms dedicated to the discussion of his ideas. Niccolò Machiavelli is more truly alive today than ever before.

TIMELINE

1469   Niccolò di Bernardo Machiavelli is born in Florence on May 3.

1498   Machiavelli is elected as second chancellor and secretary to the government.

1500   Machiavelli makes his first diplomatic mission to France and meets King Louis XII.

1502–1503   Machiavelli marries Marietta Corsini. He goes on diplomatic missions to Cesare Borgia in Romagna and Rome. He meets Leonardo da Vinci and returns with him to Florence. He makes his second diplomatic mission to France.

1506   Machiavelli makes a diplomatic mission to Rome and meets Pope Julius II. He makes his first diplomatic mission to the court of the Holy Roman Emperor Maximilian.

1510   Machiavelli makes his third mission to France.

1512   The republican government of Florence is overthrown, and the Medicis return to power. Machiavelli is dismissed from the government. Machiavelli is imprisoned and tortured after being accused of conspiracy. He retires to his farm to begin *The Discourses* and writes *The Prince*.

1515   Machiavelli begins *A Dialogue on Language*.

1517   Machiavelli completes *The Discourses*.

1518   Machiavelli writes *La Mandragola* (The Mandrake Root).

1520   Machiavelli finishes *The Art of War* and *The Life of Castruccio Castracani*. He is commissioned to write *The History of Florence*.

1521   *The Art of War* is first published.

1525   *Clizia* is first performed.

1526   Machiavelli presents *The History of Florence* to Pope Clement VII.

1527   Machiavelli dies of a stomach illness in Florence.

Glossary

Aragon A former province of northeast Spain, originally a separate kingdom.

autocrat A dictator, one who rules alone. Machiavelli generally has this type of ruler in mind when he refers to a "prince" in his works.

cardinal A senior priest in the Catholic Church, often representing the pope away from Rome. When a pope dies, the cardinals meet and elect one of their members to be the new pope.

Catholic Church At the time of the Renaissance, the only kind of Christian church in most of Europe. Its leaders claimed it to be the only true church in the world.

Christendom In the Middle Ages and Renaissance, a word to describe all the lands in the world where the people are Christians. In practice, it generally meant Europe.

confessor A Catholic priest who listens to other Catholics confess their sins and assures them of God's forgiveness. A confessor would often be a personal spiritual adviser. Machiavelli's confessor, Matteo, was a friar.

conscript A person called by the government to do military service, usually when there are not enough volunteers. Conscripts were often chosen by lottery.

ducat A gold (sometimes silver) coin. Its name derives from the Latin word meaning "belonging to a duchy." It originated in southern Italy in the twelfth century and had become an international currency by Machiavelli's time. Ducats varied in value according to when and where they were made.

duchy A state ruled by a duke. In Renaissance Italy, duchies were small independent states that were too small to be considered kingdoms. The word "duke" derives from the Latin *dux*, meaning a military commander. Many Italian duchies were founded by military leaders.

florin An Italian gold coin, originally issued in Florence. Like the ducat, similar coins of the same name but of different values were made elsewhere in Europe.

Franciscans The second of the two main orders of friars, named after their founder, Saint Francis of Assisi.

friar Man belonging to a kind of religious order founded in the thirteenth century. Not all were priests. Unlike monks, who tend to live in communities separate from the world, friars lead a similar lifestyle but are more active in the community.

heresy A belief contrary to the teachings of the Catholic Church, as defined by the popes. In the Middle Ages and Renaissance, heresy was punishable by death by burning.

Holy Roman Empire A group of states in central Europe, mostly in present-day Germany and Austria, which was a medieval attempt to reconstruct the Roman Empire of the West (there was also a Roman Empire of the East, ruled from Greece and better known as the Byzantine Empire). The Holy Roman Emperor was elected by an oligarchy of aristocrats.

Inquisition An organization in the Catholic Church formed in 1232 to detect and punish heretics. Its members were mostly Dominican and Franciscan friars.

interdict A sentence that could be pronounced by the pope on an entire country, usually to punish its ruler. The interdict forbade anyone in that country to have the benefit of the rites of the Catholic Church. This meant children could not be baptized, men and women were not allowed to marry, people could not have their sins forgiven (so if they died without confession, they might go to hell), and the dead had to be buried without a funeral. It was an extremely powerful psychological weapon. Once a ruler obeyed the pope, the sentence of interdict would be lifted.

mandrake Also known as mandragola, two kinds of stemless flowering plant with thick roots that were believed in the Middle Ages and Renaissance to have miraculous powers. They are first mentioned in the Bible.

mass The most important religious rite of the Catholic Church, in which consecrated bread and wine are believed to become the body and blood of Jesus, also known as the Eucharist, or Holy Communion.

mercenaries Freelance soldiers who sell their services for money. Most armies of Machiavelli's time were composed mainly of French, Swiss, and German mercenaries. They are rare today, for most countries follow Machiavelli's idea, borrowed from ancient history, of having an army of its own citizens.

militia An army of citizens formed to fight for their country, either as volunteers or conscripts.

monarchy A system of government in which there is a single ruler, usually for life. Sometimes known as autocracy, it does not always mean rule by a king or a queen. Machiavelli uses the word in this wider sense.

oligarchy Government by a few, usually either aristocrats or the very rich.

Ottoman Empire A dynasty ruling the Turkish Empire from the fifteenth to the twentieth centuries. Under the Ottomans, the Turkish Empire reached its height in the sixteenth century, conquering large parts of eastern Europe.

pike The standard infantry weapon in sixteenth-century European armies. It is a kind of small-bladed stabbing spear, mounted on a long shaft about 18 feet (5.5 meters) long. Although it could be used against enemy infantry, its main purpose was to defend the soldiers equipped with the slow-loading, unreliable handguns from the attacks of enemy cavalry.

preaching friar Name for a member of the Dominican Order, one of the two main orders of friars. Although all friars were preachers, preaching, along with religious scholarship, was very important to the Dominicans.

republic A system of government in which a president rules instead of a king. A republic is not always a democracy, but can be an oligarchy or an autocracy.

weir A kind of dam for controlling the flow of water along a stretch of river to prevent flooding or to power machinery.

FOR MORE INFORMATION

The Renaissance Society of America
Graduate School and University Center
City University of New York
365 Fifth Avenue, Room 5400
New York, NY 10016-4309
(212) 817-2130
e-mail: rsa@rsa.org
Web site: http://www.rsa.org

WEB SITES

Due to the changing nature of Internet
links, the Rosen Publishing Group, Inc.,
has developed an online list of Web
sites related to the subject of this
book. This site is updated regularly.
Please use this link to access the list:

http://www.rosenlinks.com/rsar/nima

FOR FURTHER READING

Caselli, Giovanni. *The Renaissance and the New World.* London: MacDonald & Co., 1985.

Curry, Patrick, and Oscar Zarate. *Introducing Machiavelli.* New York: Totem Books, 1996.

Howarth, Sarah. *Renaissance People.* New York: Simon & Schuster, 1992.

Powell, Anton. *Renaissance Italy.* London: Grisewood & Dempsey, 1979.

Wood, Tim. *The Renaissance.* Toronto: Hamlyn/Reed, 1993.

BIBLIOGRAPHY

Bock, Gisela. *Machiavelli and Republicanism.* Edited by Gisela Bock, Quentin Skinner, and Naurizio Viroli. New York: Cambridge University Press, 1990.

Gardiner, Stephen. *A Machiavellian Treatise.* Edited and translated by Peter Samuel Donaldson. New York: Cambridge University Press, 1975.

Machiavelli, Niccolò. *The Discourses.* Edited by Bernard Crick. London: Penguin Books USA Inc., 1970.

Machiavelli, Niccolò. *The Literary Works of Machiavelli: Clizia, a Dialogue on Language, Belfagor, with Selections from the Private Correspondence.* Edited and translated by J. R. Hale. Westport, CT: Greenwood Press, 1979.

Machiavelli, Niccolò. *The Living Thoughts of Machiavelli, Presented by Count Carlo Sforza.* Translated by Doris E. Troutman and Dr. Arthur Livingston. Westport, CT: Greenwood Press, 1975.

Machiavelli, Niccolò. *The Prince*. Edited by Peter Bondanella and Mark Musa. New York: Oxford University Press, 1984.

Masters, Roger D. *Fortune Is a River: Leonardo da Vinci and Niccolò Machiavelli's Magnificent Dream to Change the Course of Florentine History*. New York: The Free Press, 1998.

Ridolfi, Roberto. *The Life of Niccolò Machiavelli*. Translated by Cecil Grayson. London: Routledge and Kegan Paul, 1963.

INDEX

About the Author

Nick Ford studied comparative religion at the University of Lancaster, and gained a first-class joint honors degree from the Open University in European humanities and classical studies, then went on to postgraduate research at the University of Southampton. He has also worked as a costumed interpreter at a number of historical sites in Britain. He lives in Southampton with his wife, Carol, and two cats, Ted and Rosie.

Credits